POSITIVE DISCIPLINE FOR PARENTING PRESCHOOLERS WITH YOUR HEART & MIND

A Parenting Book Filled With Strategies & Activities To Encourage Positive Discipline

SAMANTHA EVANS

Foreword: Why You Need to Read This Book

From the moment I was pregnant, I was obsessed with parenting books. As a first time mom, I didn't know what I was going to do with this little human being that now ruled my world, even before he got here. I thought by the time he came into this world, I had better figure out some good strategies for approaching this whole parenting thing.

I thought I had a handle on things, but then the sleepless nights hit me – like a ton of bricks. Everything I thought I knew about this little guy got thrown out the window. I was at my wits end, and I got so much conflicting advice. I read and reread a lot of books on how to get your baby to sleep. I tried technique after technique and hoped something would work.

Everyone had advice for me. I was barraged with a new way to proceed at every turn. The advice didn't stop, and I welcomed any help I could get. I was exhausted, and needed to find a way to get more than a couple hours of sleep in a row. My mom friends, parents, and people at the grocery store – anybody that saw me with a baby seemed to have an opinion on what I could do with my little guy to get him to sleep more. "Don't have a quiet house, make lots of noise and then they'll learn to sleep through anything", people would tell me. "Make sure their sleeping environments are peaceful, and quiet..." I read. What was I supposed to do?

It took me awhile as a mom to find what works for me, and for my family. A lot of parenting works that way. We need to get to know our kids, seek out the best advice we can find, and then figure out (through trial and error) what works best for them. Every family is different, and every child is different.

I got through the first year, the sleepless nights, the weaning, trying solid foods for the first time, and teething. When we made it to his first birthday, it was truly a celebration. I loved the second year, as he was figuring out the world around him, in his clumsy, silly, toddler way. Yes, it was exhausting, but now, on a full nights' sleep (finally!) I could conquer the world, and my little toddler.

But when the preschool age hit (around three), I had to really think about something I had sort of been avoiding. Discipline. Here was my little guy, suddenly pushing every one of my buttons. He learned words like no, and mine, and used them, all of the time. He wanted to do everything himself, and seemed to be on his own schedule, which often conflicted with mine. He would tie his shoes one day, and refused to tie them the next (of course, when we were rushing to get out the door).

Growing up I was raised with good, wholesome, old-fashioned family values, and a wooden spoon. That was how my parents kept us on the "straight and narrow". I remember those wooden spoons that my parents used to keep us on the straight and narrow. I remember how the spoons got bigger, and thicker as we got older, with the effects on us weakening. I remember, clinching, waiting, and just getting through it. It was the way things were done back then, but I knew one thing: I wasn't going to raise my kids with this kind of punishment. I had to find another way. But, I still want to raise respectful, decent, good kids.

That's why I love the Positive Discipline movement we have in parenting today. Through lots of great research, we have found a better way to discipline and teach our kids. There are many great resources on Positive Parenting, or Positive Discipline out there. This book is a just one of them. It helped me understand a little more about what positive parenting is, and how I could guide and teach my little guy better. love

This book is filled with a lot of fun ideas to help you parent your preschooler. If you are struggling with ways to positively discipline your preschooler (and this is a tough age for all parents, right?) then you need to read this book. It takes you through a few of the common struggles we've all dealt with, and offers some great advice, strategies and activities to make things a lot easier, and more productive.

I am assuming that if you are reading this book, you care a lot about how you are going to parent and raise your kids. You have probably thought a lot about how to get your little ones listening more, and behaving better, while still keeping their autonomy. We want our little ones to express themselves, and feel safe and loved in our homes, but we also need them to move through the day, learn things and get certain things done (potty training!)

It can be a challenge to raise a preschooler. It is a time full of creativity, curiosity, stubbornness, self-centeredness, experimentation – these little ones keep you on your toes! But if you really get to see the world from their eyes, the world becomes a new and exciting place for you too.

Take some time to read this book, and try some of the tips and activities here. I love taking proactive, positive steps in raising my kids, and I'm sure you do too. I hope you find some helpful advice here in these pages, I know I did.

Thanks for reading,
Sincerely,
Samantha Evans - A mom just like you.

What is Positive Discipline?

It doesn't matter if you grew up with parents that punished you, or parents that spoiled you. Both extremes don't work in the long run. Punishment might work in the short term, and deter the bad behavior, but it certainly doesn't work in the long term.

WE HAVE LEARNED A LOT OF ABOUT RAISING HEALTHY, happy kids that go into life with positive life skills in the past few decades. The old ways of thinking and parenting need not apply. We now know that we can raise our kids to be independent thinkers, to self-motivate, and to have social skills that they can depend on in the future.

POSITIVE DISCIPLINE, OR POSITIVE PARENTING (BOTH terms are used interchangeably in this guide), is the way parents should approach parenting. We are trying to guide, educate and lead our kids to the best possible future they can have. We are not trying to demean or humiliate them, compete with them, punish them, or ignore them.

Positive Discipline is about setting your children up for a success in the future. If you want your kids to become independent, autonomous and depend on you less and less as the years go by, then you need to give them the skills to do so. Reading this guide is a great start. Here we discuss some of the simple things you can start doing today to raise healthy, independent-thinking, fun-loving kids.

Some of the tips and activities are ideas from moms and dads just like you. If you are stuck for ideas on what to do with your little one, or just at your wits end with that whiny toddler, this book will help. Just knowing that there are things that you can do, or try, helps you feel more empowered in this parenting thing.

Not every tip or strategy in this book is going to work for your family. Just remember that your family is unique, and special – You have to do what works best for your family. As parents, it is your job to know your kids, and what will or won't work when it comes to parenting. Yes, this guide is full of ideas, and strategies to help, but if something doesn't work for your family, move on and find something that does work.

But positive discipline does work for every family. Instead of punishing your kids, and succumbing to the power struggles (nobody really wins), you can guide and teach your kids, and show them how to make their own choices. We're not saying you let your kids completely off on their own. No, they need guidance, and boundaries, that you set up. Boundaries actually make them feel more secure and safe. We need to give kids structured routines, and clearly set boundaries, but they need to have some control too.

Letting your kids make their own choices is an important part of positive discipline. And there are a lot of choices you can give kids during the day. Choices like, "What color cereal bowl you want, red or blue?" "Do you want to play with puzzles or with Legos?" Many tips and strategies in this book are about ways to give your kids choices throughout the day. Kids need to feel like they have some control in their lives, if they don't, they will find ways to take it.

And kids can take control. Kids can control what goes in, and what goes out. So if you're struggling with mealtimes, or potty training, the first step is always to stop struggling.

Consistency

One of the things we will talk about a lot in this book is consistency. It isn't always easy to be consistent. But consistency isn't perfection – if you give in, and lose patience one day, all hope isn't lost.

Remember what you are trying to achieve with your kids. You want them to cooperate with you, not to obey you. You want them to have initiative, and make their own choices, within your clearly defined parameters. You want them to feel empowered in their worlds, and explore and learn because that's what they want to do.

When we give our kids the safe, structured freedom to explore and learn, letting them make choices, and giving them guidance and clear directions, we are setting them up for success. When we demean, punish, discipline, talk down to, and push our kids to comply, we aren't giving them the best chance at a successful future. We need to always keep in mind that these little people around us are, in fact, little people that someday become big people.

We will one day send them out into the world, and if we're doing our jobs right, these little people will be confident, self-motivated, and able to navigate the world around them with curiosity and passion. That is our ultimate goal, isn't it?

What Should Punishment or Discipline Be?

We never want to hit, demean, yell at or punish our kids into doing what we want them to do. Ultimately these kinds of negative punishments don't work. They might stop the behavior in the short term, but ultimately negative punishment doesn't work.

So if you can't punish your kids, what do you do? You need to find a way to teach and guide your kids, and ultimately teach them to self-regulate their behaviors. But this doesn't happen overnight, and this doesn't happen without strong, persistent parenting, and follow-through.

Just because you are not "punishing" your kids, doesn't mean you are disciplining them. Kids, especially preschoolers are always pushing the limits, trying to figure out what they should, and shouldn't do. They need strong parental guidance, strong rules and guidelines, and consistent follow-through. The best thing we can give our kids is that sense of safety and security, and nothing says security for kids like knowing what is expected of them, and what will happen if they don't do what they are supposed to.

Give your kids plenty of structure, and guidance, and be there for them when they push those boundaries. Help them navigate the world around them, and keep them safe. Positive parenting is about teaching kids social and life skills, creating an environment for them to learn, and grown. We need to keep this in mind as we move throughout our day, and try to get our little ones to listen. But what happens when they just don't seem to listen.

Some of the principles and concepts in this book come directly from,

Positive Discipline for Preschoolers, Jane Nelson, Ed.D., Cheryl Erwin, M.A., and Roslyn Ann Duffy, Harmony Books, 3rd ed., 2007

. . .

SAMANTHA EVANS

I will cite and reference this book as necessary.

Here is the list of 7 reasons why your preschooler doesn't listen, from *Positive Discipline for Preschoolers*. Here they are:

1. Adults yell, lecture, or nag, which doesn't invite listening.

2. Adults don't ask a child what she should or should not be doing, but *tell* her.

3. Adults set up power struggles that make winning more important than cooperating.

4. The child is "programmed" by her instinct towards development to explore—and the adult doesn't want her to. The voice of a child's instinct is usually louder than the voice of an adult.

5. The child cannot comply with a request because it demands social skills or thinking skills that have not yet developed.

6. Children don't have the same priorities as adults.

. . .

7. ADULTS DON'T LISTEN TO CHILDREN.

IF YOU WANT YOUR PRESCHOOLER TO REALLY LISTEN TO you, then you to really listen to them. Don't just wait for your turn to retell them what you want them to do, or bark another order at them. This isn't always easy. When we are rushing out the door, have somewhere to go, something to do, or it's bedtime, we just want our little one to comply and move along. But they don't always. They are their own little people, with their own ideas, personalities and temperaments. They have plans of their own, and we should respect that.

YES, WE NEED TO GIVE THEM ROUTINES, STRUCTURES, AND rules to follow, but we also need to value their input. We need to stop trying to accomplish each task throughout the day, and focus on what's really important: raising our kids.

How this book is structured:

MANY OF THE TIPS, STRATEGIES AND ACTIVITIES COME FROM real parents just like you. They have been proven in the real world, and have worked for them. Every tip, strategy and idea that is here isn't going to work for you. Take what you need, and leave the rest for someone else.

THE BOOK STARTS WITH THE FIRST CHAPTER, 8 WAYS TO Become a Positive Parent. This chapter gives you some ways to quickly incorporate positive parenting into your life today.

These are the overriding principles that you need to keep in your mind as you move and groove through this parenting journey.

Next the book is organized into more specific chapters that can be easily referenced for when you need them. This is where you can find the specific tips and strategies that you need. Here is a brief overview of these chapters:

8 Ways to Become a Positive Parent

So by now you're on board to becoming a positive parenting. Before we get the specific strategies and activities that you can do, here are 8 ways to become a positive parent in any situation. These are the foundation to positive parenting. Keep in mind these fundamental principles as you go through your days with your kids.

I BELIEVE THAT IF YOUR INTENTION IS TO PARENT positively, and you keep in mind these 8 overriding principles, you will have much more success. The following chapters will give you more specific ideas, and strategies that you can use in any situation, but you should always come back to these basic positive discipline principles.

(FROM *POSITIVE DISCIPLINE FOR PRESCHOOLERS*, PG. 14)

8 METHODS FOR IMPLEMENTING POSITIVE DISCIPLINE

1. Get children involved:
2. In the creation of routines
3. Through the use of limited choices
4. By providing opportunities to help

1. Teach respect by being respectful

1. Use your sense of humor

1. Get into your child's world

1. Say what you mean, and then follow through with kindness and firmness

1. Be patient

1. Act, don't talk—and supervise carefully

1. Accept and appreciate your child's uniqueness

GET CHILDREN INVOLVED.

1. *In the creation of routines*
2. *Through the use of limited choices*
3. *By providing opportunities to help*

CHILDREN NEED TO FEEL LIKE THEY HAVE SOME CONTROL over their lives. "Instead of telling children what to do, find ways to involve them in decisions and to draw out what they think and perceive". When we involve our kids in our day-to-day lives, they feel like they have more control, and power over their worlds. Over time, this builds their self-esteem, and ability to make choices on their own.

KIDS NEED ROUTINES, AND BY GETTING THEM INVOLVED BY helping to choose their routines, they get to understand the natural consequences of their choices. We do need to provide limited choices, however for our kids. It is through repetition and consistency that they will learn new skills. We need to create opportunities for them to grow and learn, every day. By providing opportunities to help us throughout the day, our kids will learn what it takes to be a "grown up". Kids revel in learning, for them it really is an exciting adventure. Don't take these learning opportunities away from your kids by scheduling and doing every thing for them. Sometimes the learning is slow, and messy, but that's okay. Get used to messy, and slow.

Teach respect by being respectful

Listen to your children. Figure out what their needs are, and respect their little personalities. Some kids need lots of breaks, and quiet time during the day. Some kids thrive when there is a lot to do, and want to play with other kids. Know your child, and respect who they are. Respect their timelines, their needs, their schedules and unique temperaments. Our kids are special, and learn and move in the world on their own terms. Celebrate that.

Use your sense of humor

Sometimes parenting seems like such serious business. And, you are serious about wanting the best for your children, and giving them the best start in life. But kids are kids, and they need to not only feel safe, they need to have fun. A child's life should be full of fun moments, and lots and lots of laughter. Sometimes we take our parenting role so seriously, we forget to just lighten up and laugh with our kids. It can be a lot easier to get our little ones to do something if we make a game of it, and have a sense of humor when things go wrong. And things will go wrong.

Get into your child's world

How do we truly connect with our children? At

times it seems like they are living in completely separate worlds than us, but we still have to get through to them. We need to have empathy and understanding for our little ones. We need to try to understand their perspectives, and respect how they are feeling. Preschoolers have complicated emotions at times, and can often react to situations dramatically. We need to get down to our child's level, really listen to them and try to understand where they are coming from.

Say what you mean, and then follow through with kindness and firmness

Positive Discipline is not about giving your child everything that they want. Permissiveness doesn't help your child develop initiative, or other social skills that they need. What you need to do, instead, is offer clearly defined choices and follow through on these choices with kindness and firmness. And, yes, you need to be consistent with your efforts. If you give them two choices, don't let them make up a third choice. Make sure choices are appropriate, not only for their age, and development level, but also for their individual personalities. Again, we need to get to know and respect our little ones unique place in this world, and start from there when we proceed into each day.

Be patient

We all know that kids are not our little programmable robots. And, we don't really want them to be either. They come into this world with their own temperaments, personality, likes and dislikes. They won't always agree with us, and as they get older, they want to do things their own way more and more.

If we can truly empathize with our kids – see the world from their perspective, through their eyes – we will automatically be more patient with them. The world is a big, scary, yet awesomely fascinating place for a little one. They are always being told what they cannot do, what they should be doing, and how they should act. At times, this can become overwhelming for them, and until they can learn how to cope, and self-regulate (something we will address later on in this book) all of the time, there will be meltdowns. And I can't think of a time when our patience is tested than during a meltdown.

But this is exactly the time when our little ones need us. Once they are in full-blown-meltdown mode they lose all ability to think rationally, or self-soothe. Their brains just shut down. We need to know (where the patience comes from), that this will pass. There are some proactive things that we can do to help prevent these rough patches, but when we're in the middle of the meltdown, there isn't much we can do, except be patient, and try to get them to focus on something else. In the next chapter we will give you some more examples of what to do to avoid meltdowns in the first place, and also what to do when we are faced with a meltdown.

Act, don't talk—and supervise carefully

. . .

There is a reason why parenting is so tough and exhausting for most of us. Today's parent feels like they have to be on high alert all of the time when it comes to supervising their little ones. It can be so frustrating when you feel like you can't walk away from your little one playing, even for a minute or two, just in case something messy, or even worse, dangerous happens. But we need to let our little ones learn and play, without our hovering. We can guide them to a more acceptable place, but we need to give them enough freedom to learn on their own too.

Accept and Appreciate Your Child's Uniqueness

We have discussed this a lot so far, but isn't it important? Our kids not only need to be accepted for who they are, they need to be celebrated for who they are. We need to fan the flames of their unique interests, and give them toys, and activities that we know they will love, not just set them up with what we think they should play with. Not all kids will love sports or structured activities. Some kids are natural artists, or creative-types. We need to get to know what makes our kids special, and then do everything in our power to provide them the experiences that will make them happy.

The Basics

Here you will find some more specific examples and activities to build positive parenting into your lives. These tips were from parents just like you.

Strategies and Activities: The Basics

Here you will find some more specific examples and activities to build positive parenting into your lives. These tips were from parents just like you.

1. **Build on your own child's unique strengths.**

Some kids are natural talkers, and some kids are super active. Building on your child's natural strengths lets them feel good about themselves, and strengthens their self-esteem. But building on their strengths, instead of harboring on their weaknesses. If they haven't learned their letters and numbers yet, but they are really good at art, let them express themselves through art. You can still work on numbers and letters, but don't forget about the art.

1. **Enjoy the process of learning with your children.**

Don't always have a goal in mind of what you want to accomplish. Kids enjoy the process of learning, and don't need to know where they are headed. We, as parents, and adults are much more project-oriented. If we aren't getting something accomplished, why are we doing it at all? But kids don't think this way, they enjoy the journey, the process much more than we do. Enjoy the learning, and details along the way.

1. **Get them involved in *your* day to day lives.**

You spend so much time scheduling their little lives, and finding fun, educational activities that you think they will benefit from. But the funny thing about kids, especially preschoolers – they want to be just like you. They want to do what you do everyday. Get your kids involved in making meals, cleaning (not just their own toys), shopping – all those things that make up our day-to-day lives. They might not seem so glamorous and exciting to us. But these things can be so exciting and fun for our kids.

1. **Stock up, and be ready, for anything. Really.**

There is a reason why parents need to carry around a big bag of stuff. You never know when you are going to need something for your kids to eat, to do, or to play with. Make sure you are always carrying something that will temporarily entertain or distract them. You'll thank yourself when you unexpectedly have to wait in that extra long line at the shop.

1. **Visual schedules. Use pictures and words.**

Kids learn things and build important pathways in their brains through their five senses. When we talk to them, and ask them to do something, we are only engaging one of the five senses. This can be tough for little ones, who are still figuring out the world around them.

We want to tell them what is expected of them, but we also need to show them. Visual aids, or visual schedules are great for this. If you want your little one to sit and eat lunch, then have playtime, all you need to do is create a small picture of "lunch", and a small picture of "toys". Use these to get through those tough transitions throughout the day too.

1. **Get down on their level to see the world.**

While it is important to get down on the mat to play with your kids, it is just as important to look around at the world from their level. What does their world look like from that vantage point? Remember what their world looks like as you move and groove throughout the day. Put in a step stool so they can wash their own hands. Make sure they have access to their toys, and can easily put them away. Get down on their level when you want to get their attention too.

1. **Know what is age-appropriate for your child.**

What age can you expect them to empathize? To share? To be able to sit for circle time? To use the potty independently?

That depends. There are general guidelines and milestone charts that you can access to find out what should be age-appropriate for your child, but they are just guidelines. You have to know (and get to know) your own child's abilities. Figure out if they understand the concept of sharing, and the mechanics of it before you expect them to naturally do so.

1. **Remember to celebrate even the very small steps.**

Kids can take a long time to learn something new, or to change a behavior. We forget this sometimes, especially if we are comparing our kids to our friends' kids. We think they need to hit every milestone early, or right on time and if they don't, we didn't do something right. Kids' learning isn't always as linear as we'd like to think it is. It is up and down, and up and down. It is slow.

This can be especially true when it comes to potty training. We've all heard the stories of kids that were potty trained in a day. But this isn't always the case. There are accidents, and setbacks, and sometimes all-out refusals to potty at all. Sometimes we need to stop focusing on the end goal, and just celebrate the small steps along the way.

1. **Who am I? Let your kids find out for themselves.**

Don't waste your time, energy and resources buying your kids toys that you think they should enjoy. Boys' toys or girls' toys? Does it really matter? Educational toys? Are they really necessary? What kind of toys does your child naturally gravitate towards? Let them be your guide when it comes to providing a fun-filled environment for them to explore.

1. **Build new skills with child-specific charts.**

When trying to teach a child a new skill, such as getting dressed, without your help in the morning, you need to start with the small steps. A good way to remind and teach your little ones these steps is to make a picture chart detailing each step they need to do. Go through each step with them a few times, and gradually let them figure it out on their own. Eventually, you'll want them to be able to do each step, successfully, on their own, without any prompting and help from you.

1. **Praise specifically. Give encouragement, not just praise.**

Encouraging your kids should be specific to what they are doing, not just random "good jobs" throughout the day. Let them know that you acknowledge they are trying, and accomplishing new tasks, by specifically telling them how good they are doing that new task.

1. **Know and acknowledge your child's unique temperament.**

There are nine different temperaments that shape your child's personality and how they move and act throughout their day (Positive Discipline for Preschoolers, pg. 101)

1. Activity Level
2. Rhythmically
3. Initial Response (approach or withdrawal)
4. Adaptability
5. Sensory threshold
6. Quality of mood
7. Intensity of reactions
8. Distractibility
9. Persistence and attention span

You don't need to know what all of these mean, but if you want to look them up, you should. Just know that every child has his or her own way of seeing, acting and moving around in the world. Take the time to get to know their unique temperament in any situation. What kind of temperament do you have? Weren't you the same as a child? Don't work against their temperaments: work with them.

1. **Schedule time for yourself.**

I know with little ones around, time for you is a luxury. But it really shouldn't be. You need to have the energy, and mental acuteness to take care of these little ones. And, they are demanding. They need your time, attention, direction and encouragement. You need to find ways to take care of yourself. Ask for help, and schedule time away from your little ones. Do things that you enjoy, and look forward to. Don't wait until your little ones are ready, or in bed. Schedule time everyday that makes you feel better.

1. **Practice active listening with your kids.**

Don't just wait until they are done to tell them what you want. Listen to what they are telling you, and tell them you hear them, even if you don't always agree with them. Find ways to make sure they know that you are listening to them, and acknowledging what they want. Most of the time we are so busy getting through the day, we forget to really listen to them. If you cannot repeat back what your child just said, you need to work on active listening.

Positive Time Outs

Here we go. How do you discipline your little one? What is a positive time out, and how can I start giving them to my child? Here you will get some great tips on what to do to avoid the meltdowns from happening in the first place, but also tips on what to do when meltdowns occur.

Strategies and Activities: Positive Time-Outs

Here we go. How do you discipline your little one? What is a positive time out, and how can I start giving them to my child? Here you will get some great tips on what to do to avoid the meltdowns from happening in the first place, but also tips on what to do when meltdowns occur.

1. Change punishments to positive time-outs.

Forget everything you think you know about time-outs if it's negative. Time-outs can be a great tool for raising our kids, if we change the old notions of punishment, and struggle. Sometimes, when it comes to parenting, we need to think about what we are doing, and ask ourselves, it is working?

We all think that time-outs consist of negative punishments, having the child sit in the corner, or forcing them out of the room for a designated amount of time. There are countless parenting experts that support the time-out method, especially for preschoolers. But, have you ever tried this method? It can be filled with frustrations, piled on frustrations as you try to force your little one to sit, and stay seated, staring at a wall, while you set a timer to correspond to their age. Two minutes for a two year-old, three minutes for a three year-old, etc.

Time outs don't have to be this painful and arduous at all. How would you feel if you were having a stressful day, felt frustrated, and instead of being able to move onto something more enjoyable, or simply take a break from what was frustrating you, someone made you sit still for 28 minutes? This wouldn't work for us, but somehow we think this is the way we need to discipline our kids. But, it isn't.

Discipline actually means 'to teach', and that, ultimately is what we want to do to our kids. We want them to learn what is appropriate behavior, how to self-regulate emotions, and actions, and how to give themselves breaks, if they need them.

Positive discipline for preschoolers isn't about punishment, or negative consequences. It is about creating an environment that kids will thrive, and learn how to regulate their own behaviors. With positive time outs, kids get the much needed break from their negative behaviors, or meltdowns, and can learn (with your patience, and guidance), that they can move on to something more productive.

Here are some activities and strategies to create positive time outs for your preschoolers, and defuse those meltdowns.

1. **Know what causes meltdowns in your little ones, and try to avoid it.**

Finding out what causes the meltdown is the first step. If you are dealing with a little one that has a lot of meltdowns, become your own detective. Track what time the meltdown started, how long it lasted, and what you think it could be about. Keep a meltdown log, and refer back to it for reference. Now, do some detective work. Are the meltdowns always happening before naptime, when your little one is tired? If so, could you move nap time back a bit to avoid the meltdown.

The best way to deal with meltdowns is to prevent them from happening in the first place. Discover what triggers, or sets off the meltdowns, and strategize a way to avoid this from happening.

Sometimes, though, no matter how much planning, tracking and strategizing we do, we can't avoid the preschooler meltdowns. When meltdowns occur, you need to help your little one navigate their own way out of that. This is not the time to tell them what they are doing wrong, or to try to teach them a new skill.

Think about the meltdown as the top of mountain. The lead up to the mountain is not a quick climb (although it can seem that way), and the way down the mountain takes time too. That's how the meltdown works for our little ones. There is always something leading up to the meltdown – hunger, tiredness, someone wouldn't share with them, they are hurt, angry, sad, upset – and there is always a time period to cool down from the meltdown. That's where positive cool-down time outs can help, in getting kids down that meltdown mountain.

1. **Create a positive space or corner that kids can sit in, to cool-down.**

Find a corner, or a small space in your house that works best for you and make it your child's "cool-down" or "chill out" space. Put a beanbag chair, or some big, comfy pillows, and maybe a few books. Don't fill it up with toys. This is a space that you'll send them to when they are being over-stimulated, frustrated and just need some cooling off time.

1. **Get a squishy, squeeze ball for time-outs to help with tension and stress.**

Find a ball or something they can squish, and focus on when they are in time out. Sometimes kids need to feel that deep pressure in their hands to cool down. Experiment with what works best for your little ones.

1. **Make a time-out bottle.**

Some parents like to make time out bottles, and these can work well too. Take a water bottle, fill it with sparkly stuff, and maybe a few small toys, or colored water. Hot glue the top back on, and give them this to focus on when they are in time out. The bottle can be a great way to hold their direction on something while they cool off, and settle down. You can also take these time-out bottles with you, so you don't need to send them to their corner to calm down. Just pull it out of your fully packed arsenal when you need them to self-regulate.

1. **Stop and give them some pictures to focus on.**

Sometimes when little ones are stuck at the top of that meltdown mountain, it seems nothing will help them down. But know this, when they are in the middle of the meltdown, their minds do just shut down. The first step to getting them out of that space can be just to get them to focus on anything else. Sometimes a series of still pictures, try google images, or online photo files to get help with this. Take out your smart phone or tablet, and scroll through pictures of flowers, eggs, trees, sunsets with them. Wait for them to focus on the pictures, and start the climb down the meltdown mountain from there.

1. **Let them move onto something else.**

Redirection is a great tool for preschoolers. If you see some behavior that you don't like, try redirecting them onto something you do like. Change rooms, change toys, change something, and see if that works. Remember preschoolers don't usually have long attention spans. Take advantage of their short attention spans, and try redirection first.

1. **Now could be a good time for some tech time.**

Kids today love their gadgets, even preschoolers seem to navigate through a smart phone, or tablet with ease. Yes, you should limit their tech time, but you shouldn't take it away from them completely. Sometimes a tablet, or a smart phone can offer that much needed focused break for your little one that could become another positive time out tactic for you to try. Let them watch a few kid-friendly songs, or videos, or play an educational game. This focus on something new (and limited) could get your little one out of that soon-to-be meltdown stage quickly, and quietly.

1. **Catch them in the act of being good, and super-praise them.**

Teaching them new skills, or changing a behavior in a preschooler can often take time. But instead of scolding them, or correcting them when they do wrong, we need to focus on what they are doing right. For example, your preschooler is always poking at, and kicking your family dog.

This is undesirable, negative behavior that needs to stop. Instead of always shouting "no" or "stop that" when the bad behavior starts, try catching them when they are being nice to the dog, and super-praise them to pieces. Wait, and find another time they are being good to the dog, and super-praise them all over again. Positive attention is just as rewarding as negative attention for a preschooler. Make sure they get lots, and lots of positive attention.

Mealtimes

Mealtimes don't have to be a source of stress and panic. Stop the tug of war with your little ones, and get them involved. Start making mealtimes a pleasurable part of your day that your whole family can share.

Strategies and Activities: Mealtimes

Mealtimes don't have to be a source of stress and panic. Stop the tug of war with your little ones, and get them involved. Start making mealtimes a pleasurable part of your day that your whole family can share.

1. **Mealtimes – Dealing with picky eaters. Some specific strategies.**

If you have a picky eater, you could have a problem on your hands. One area that kids have full control is in what goes in their mouth. They are ultimately the ones that decide what they want to eat, how much they want to eat, and when they are going to eat. What do you do if you find yourself with a picky eater? First, don't panic. There are lots of things you could do to help move things along.

1. Don't overwhelm with too big of portion sizes. Kids have tiny little stomachs, and often eat such small portions we wonder how they can grow at all.
2. Always offer them something they love to eat.

Don't starve your kids, or punish them for not liking certain things. There are many reasons why a kid won't eat something. You still want them to eat.

3. Offer them the foods you want them to eat at every meal, but in very, very small amounts. Don't overwhelm them with a big bunch of broccoli, or a bunch of cooked carrots on their plates if they don't want to eat them. Offer one tiny little piece of carrot at a time, and ask them to try it.
4. Small steps count. If your picky eater is willing to touch a new, or strange food, great! Start there. Work with that. Will they try a small nibble next time? Great. Celebrate each small success.
5. Try dips, and sauces to dip fruit and vegetables into. Ranch dressing, real maple syrup, even caramel sauce and ketchup all might help get your little one tasting and eating fruits and veggies.
6. Don't fool them. Hiding vegetables in sauces and casseroles doesn't always work if they don't like the strong taste to begin with. If you want them to get used to a certain flavor of vegetables, then add a small amount to their foods, and slowly adjust until they are used to that flavor.
7. Be a good example. Eat your vegetables, protein and fruits. Let your kids try things off their plates, just make sure what's on your plate is healthy.
8. **Get kids to sit and eat.**

Kids are full of energy and sometimes this energy spills over into meal times. While you want them to be full of life, and excited about their days, you also want them to sit still, and enjoy a family meal. There are things you can do to make mealtimes more enjoyable for everyone.

1. **Pick your mealtime battles.**

What do you want mealtimes to look like? Do you imagine a happy, quiet family, silently enjoying the beautiful food, and then quickly clearing off their plates afterwards? This isn't what most family meals look like. Most family meals are rushed, and busy. Kids can either eat really, really slow, or really, really fast. Some kids are non-stop talkers, and never eat their food, while others are non-stop eaters, and don't want to talk. What do you want your family meals to be like? Keep in mind— this is your family we're talking about.

1. **Find good reasons to stay at the table.**

If you want your kids to stay longer at the table, give them a reason (motivation) to do so. Let them play with a quiet toy. Ask them a bunch of questions about their day. Tell funny stories, or jokes. Have a good time too.

24. **Get them involved in meal preparations:**
Can they mix the salad? Pick the salad dressings? Pick the color of plates they get to use? Set the table? Decide where everyone gets to sit? Let them be a part of the family meal, before the actual sit-down portion as much as possible.

1. **Let them eat cake! And, decide what game to play!**

Giving kids some really fun choices in their lives is a great way to encourage cooperation. Life can get super serious sometimes, and we all know that kids aren't very good at being super serious. Let them be kids! Let them have cake for breakfast today. Make sure they know that this is a special occasion. Let them choose a family fun activity to do today.

Not all choices have to be tough, or goal-oriented. Sometimes we get to make super fun choices too.

1. **Give them their own kitchen and fridge drawers.**

Stop fighting over snack times, and meal preparations with your kids. Set up healthy snack drawers in your pantry and fridge that kids are welcome to pick freely from. If you want them to have set limits to certain items, then label them: choose 1, choose 2, choose as many as you want. Stock them up with healthy choices, and give them free reign to enjoy. You could also get kids to pack, or make their own breakfasts, and lunches using this method.

Potty Training

Why are we still talking about potty training with your preschooler? For those of you that haven't conquered this step yet with your little one (and there are lots of you out there), here are some quick tips and strategies to get you through this milestone.

Strategies and Activities: Potty Training

※

Potty training might be something you have already conquered, and if so, phew! But if you haven't, don't worry. You are not alone. A lot of kids don't get fully potty trained until they are in their third year. So please, try not to stress too much. There are many good resources on potty training that might help (provided below), but we'll just go through a few tips and tricks that might just help you break through this milestone.

Some Great Potty Training Resources:

Stress-Free Potty Training: A Commonsense Guide to Finding the Right Approach for Your Child, Peter L. Stavinoha, Sara Au, May 28, 2008, Trade Paperback

It's No Accident: Breakthrough Solutions To Your Child's Wetting, Constipation, Utis, And Other Potty Problems, Steve J. Hodges, Suzanne Schlosberg, February 7, 2012, Paperback

The No-Cry Potty Training Solution: Gentle Ways to Help Your Child Say Good-Bye to Diapers, Elizabeth Pantley, August 28, 2006, Paperback

1. **Let them decide when they are ready.**

This can be a tough one for parents, who often have imposed potty-training deadlines (starting school, preschool, before the next child comes home). But kids need to feel like they have some control over their lives, and one area they have control is toileting. Fighting and struggling over this issue can literally backfire on you.

If your little one is having trouble pooping, and withholding it, you won't be able to potty train very easily. You should see your doctor to get some advice if this happening, it could require some medical intervention. If you suspect that your child is ready to be potty training, but is withholding poops, hiding in other rooms to poop, or showing signs of fear and anxiety around pooping, please see a doctor.

1. **Keep potty training fun and exciting.**

Once they show some interest in potty training, run with it. Show them how much fun the potty can be. Bring in some noise-makers, stickers, music, books – anything to make a potty party fun. Have a big celebration when your little one goes on the potty. Make it a game, a fun one that they'll want to play over and over again.

1. **Are they ready physically and mentally?**

We need to respect our kids' individual time line when it comes to reaching those milestones. Not all kids will be ready, either physically or mentally for potty training, when we think they should be. Some kids just need extra time, and a little growing up to do before they will be ready for potty training.

If they cannot tell when they have to pee, they are not physically ready for potty training yet. Just wait. If they have any cognitive delays, speech delays, or other issues, they might not be ready to potty train yet. Ask your doctor if you have any concerns, especially if you think there could be some reasons for the delays.

1. **Make your own potty training book.**

A lot of kids are visual learners. Having pictures of their own can help them to understand the steps they need accomplish. Take pictures of your little ones on the potty, playing with toilet paper, flushing the potty – make a book with their pictures, pictures of other kids on the potty, and detail all the steps that they need to take. Get them involved in the making of the book. They can glue and add their own pictures, stickers, etc. and help create their own potty book. Let them use this not only as a guide, but also as a 'brag book' so that they can brag about their toilet accomplishments that day.

1. **Don't worry. It will happen.**

Let us remember that just because they haven't hit this milestone, doesn't mean it will never happen. Remember even a delay is just a delay, not a permanent. One day your child will be potty trained. Hang in there and know that you are doing everything you can to help them learn, but don't beat yourself up if your child doesn't master this right away.

1. **It can take a long time for a child to be "fully" potty trained.**

Think about all the learning that has to happen for a child to be fully potty trained. They have to recognize the sensations of pee and poop, know how to pull their pants down, sit on the seat, wait until they are done on the toilet, wipe themselves (often a tough task for little ones), flush the toilet, pull their pants back up, wash their hands, and dry their hands. They have to be able to tell an adult they have to go if they are in daycare or preschool, and if not, they have to make their own way to the bathroom in their house.

There are a lot of steps along the way in potty training, and these can take months and months to master. Don't worry if your little one still needs help wiping, or washing their hands properly. These steps will come. Focus on the steps they are doing properly, celebrate these steps, and move on from there.

1. **Don't let others push this issue. Don't compare your child to others.**

Sometimes it seems like every child other than yours is already potty trained, and I'm sure your parents forgot how tough potty training actually was. People don't often share the nitty-gritty tough parts of their lives, and it seems like potty training is so easy for everyone, except you. Potty training can often be a lengthy, tough, trial-and-error process. Don't let others timelines change you and your child's timeline. They all learn at different speeds.

Bedtime Routines

Most parents will have to deal with bedtime and sleep routine issues at some point with their preschooler. This is the time when they might stop taking naps altogether (if they haven't already) and could mean disruptions at night. If you have more than one child, this could mean more changes at night too. Here are some simple, effective things you can do to create a fun bedtime routine that your little one will look forward to every night.

Strategies and Activities: Bedtime Routines

Most parents will have to deal with bedtime and sleep routine issues at some point with their preschooler. This is the time when they might stop taking naps altogether (if they haven't already) and could mean disruptions at night. If you have more than one child, this could mean more changes at night too. Here are some simple, effective things you can do to create a fun bedtime routine that your little one will look forward to every night.

1. **Let them make choices at bedtime too.**

Let them decide some of the order of things at bedtime. They can read one book, then brush their teeth, and then read another book. They can choose their own books.

1. **Be silly.**

Read to your kids in silly voices. Become a scary tickle monster, and chase your kids through the house. Let them hang upside down. Jump up and down with your kids and count how many times you can before you both get tired.

1. **Bedtime battles. You won't win if you make bedtime a battle. You cannot make kids fall asleep.**

There really is no "off button" for our kids. They will sleep, but usually not when you want them too. Some kids are excellent sleepers, and love their beds, and naps. Some kids fight sleep with every fiber of their little bodies, and kick and scream their way into slumber. How do you help your little ones get enough sleep, and fall asleep on their own, without your help? Keep reading...

1. **Create a flexible, kids choose themselves bedtime routine.**

Let your kids help decide (with you) parts of their own bedtime routines. There are lots of ways they can get involved in the making and implementing of the bedtime routine. Here are some ideas to get them involved. There are many bedtime routine possibilities: (From *Positive Discipline for Preschoolers*, pg 220)

1. **Playtime, at bedtime.**

Let them choose the after dinner, before bed playtime activity with your family. Give them their own day to pick an activity that you all do. Some families like to put on some music and dance together. Some families prefer quiet board game the whole family can play. Give them a set time, say 45 minutes, and give them two or three choices, and let them decide. Make family playtime a fun, interactive part of your bedtime routine.

1. **Small choices along the way.**

Give your kids as many of the small choices along the way as you can, especially at bedtime. Let them choose the pajamas they will wear or what books they get to read at story time. When they are little, you can give them the choice from two or three of your choices, but as they get bigger, you can let them have more freedom. If they choose to wear summer pajamas to bed in the winter: no problem. If they want to read one really long book at story time: no problem. Let them make their own choices and try to support them in them. They will develop the skills to make better choices, only if you give the autonomy to make them.

1. **Make bath time an option. Maybe shower time?**

Bath time doesn't have to happen every night, but it can be a great way to wind down, and relax before bed. Let your kids take showers if they prefer. Give your kids the option of which soap to use, which shampoo they want, and what toys they want in the tub. Let them play with the running water too, most of them really like that, and it makes the bath last that much longer (especially if the water is running really slow).

1. **Tooth brushing. Make this fun.**

Who says brushing your teeth can't be fun? Sing funny tooth brushing songs, or take turns with your little ones brushing each other's teeth. Buy special kids toothbrushes and toothpastes that they love. You can get electric, singing toothbrushes for kids now. Let them brush their own teeth first, then check to make sure they did a good job.

1. **Story time. Reading to, and with your kids at bedtime is something you really need to do.**

I think everyone agrees that there is no bedtime routine without story time. Reading to your kids is such a great way to connect to them, to find out what they love, how their day was, and has so many benefits to their little brains.

You don't have to just read books to your kids at story time though, (and hopefully, you read to your kids more than just once a day). You can get your kids to read their favorite books to you. Most kids memorize their favorite books early on, and love to go over their favorite parts with you.

Introduce new books all the time, and see what new ones they will love. Don't forget about the public library, with loads of new books you can borrow, for free.

Be silly. Read the books in new, funny voices. Sing parts of the books. Make up new stories along the way. Encourage your little ones to make up their own stories too.

1. **Special Activities. Don't rush to get the kids to bed. Take the time (that they have your full attention) to build family bonds.**

Since kids are snuggled in their beds, and you have their full attention, now could be a great time to instill family values, talk about what matters to you, ask them about their days, or pray.

Take this time to build in some special time that you share with your children. Mom and dad both need to put the kids to bed if at all possible so that nobody misses out on this special bonding time.

If your kids know that at the end of the day they will get some special one on one time with you, they will soon learn to look forward to bedtime. Don't rush to finish the day, and get back to your tasks.

1. **Give your kids lots of hugs and kisses.**

Don't forget to give your kids lots of physical affection. Tell them that you love them, sure, but always show them. Play a kiss and hug counting game, or ask them how many big hugs they want. Make it fun.

Sometimes kids will use hugs and kisses at bedtime to get you to stay longer, and thus, push their bedtime routine back. I say, don't rush, but eventually, they do need to get their sleep too. That's when you give them a choice. Do you want 2 more kisses, or 2 more hugs before mommy leaves and you go to sleep?

1. **Lights out...?**

Sometimes kids like complete darkness at night; sometimes they need a night light. Give them a choice, and say good night.

Sometimes kids need some winding down time still in bed, on their own. Let them read, or play with toys in their beds at night if you want. As long as they play or read quietly, this shouldn't be a problem. Don't let them watch television though; this won't help in the long run.

Toys and books are great things to have in bed with your kids. If they have things to play with they might even stay in their beds for a little longer in the morning, giving you a little, much needed rest.

You can also help with the morning routine by clearly defining what you want your little ones to do in the morning, starting with when to wake you up. Tell them they can play quietly or read first thing in the morning, then wake you up. Try to give them time to do this by not getting up for them on the first call to you.

Playtime!

Most of a preschoolers' day will be spent in play mode, and that's how it should be. It is through play that they build new skills, and brain functions. It is through play they learn the social, and functional world around them. We need to not only include lots and lots of playtime into our preschoolers' day; we need to find ways to play with them every day too.

Strategies and Activities: Playtime!

Most of a preschoolers' day will be spent in play mode, and that's how it should be. It is through play that they build new skills, and brain functions. It is through play how they learn the social, and functional world around them. We need to not only include lots and lots of playtime into our preschoolers' day; we need to find ways to play with them every day too.

1. **Don't hurry. Take the time to enjoy an extra long walk through the park, or to let your child play in the leaves until they want to stop.**

We always seem to be rushing ourselves, and our kids from place to place, through their busy schedules, and often forget what's really important. Sometimes you will have to be late for the next dance class. If they ask for a reason, just tell them you were enjoying watching your little one...

1. **Don't rush in to fix how your child is playing.**

Stand back and observe how your child is playing. Find a way to get involved with their games, and toys, and then interject yourself into their worlds. We often think that puzzles need to be solved, or blocks need to be stacked, and dollies need to be fed. Kids will find all sorts of new and neat ways to play with their toys. Watch them, and find a way to get involved with how they are playing.

1. **Take the time to build a fort.**

Kids love when you get to destroy the living room furniture, and they love little spaces of their own. Don't just wait for a rainy day to build one either. Make a fort outside with your kids, and some blankets. Let me take naps, eat snacks and play in their forts all day. Try to get inside with them, and enjoy!

1. **Don't wait to have special adventure days with your kids.**

When my friend was little he had to have a series of tests, and operations. It turns out he had childhood cancer. Each time they had to go to the kids' hospital in the big city, his mom would make it a special day for the two of them. He got to eat at a new restaurant, take the subway, and pick out a new toy afterwards. Of course his mom was trying to make the most of this scary, unpleasant and stressful of situation by making it fun and exciting for him. And it worked. Every year he looked forward to going to the big city, to get his tests done and have that special time with new adventures with his mom.

Life is full of humdrum, busy days. We need to give our kids these special breaks too. Take them somewhere new, let them try new foods, and make it all about them. Then give them a time down the road where they can look forward to another special day with you. We all need something (other than the holidays) to look forward to.

1. **Paint a paper wall, with flying sponges.**

You can do this activity outside (or inside if you put a drop sheet down for the inevitable mess). Grab a big sheet of packing paper, some sponges and some paint. Let your little one dip the sponges in the watered-down paint, and throw them at the big sheet of paper. See what kind of art you can create. Better yet – throw some sponges yourself. It is fun. Let them hang their own creation up in their room. You can also invite a few kids over and make this a fun activity for everyone.

1. **Make double use of your kids' toys with Sensory Bins.**

Sensory bins are something that daycares, and preschools use all the time, and can be easy to make at home to use as well. Just get a big bin, or plastic container, and fill it with rice, lentils, leaves, or any kind of material that you want. Let the kids help make the sensory bin, and add in new objects or toys that they want.

There are lots of different kinds of sensory bins, and you could really let your imagination and creativity run wild with these. If you need some ideas, you can always find lots on Pinterest. Just search "sensory bins", and you will find a lot of resources.

But here are some ideas to get you started:

Make a safari sensory bin. Fill up a big container with leaves, grass, and lentils (for the sand). Add in some plastic safari animals, some jeeps, and cars, and let the kids explore the new world you have just created.

Make a winter-themed sensory bin. Roll out some toilet paper, or use white tissue paper for the bottom of the bin. Fill sections with big and small cotton balls. Let your kids add their favorite little people characters, and play in their newly created winter wonderland.

1. **Take away toys. Let them be bored. It won't last long.**

Kids are natural innovators, and if given the chance are very good at entertaining themselves. Sometimes we give our kids too many ways to entertain and teach themselves, and we lost their inherent ability to search out, and come up with ideas of their own.

1. **Play mommy and daddy with them.**

Kids are natural mimics, and they really look up to you. They want to be mommy or daddy, and will get really excited if you let them do what you do.

Stand them up on a stool, and let them wash dishes with you. Sure you will probably get the floor all wet, and not a single dish clean, but they will love the experience.

Give them a small broom, a small dustpan and let them clean the floors.

Let them (and encourage them) to do easy, simple chores around the house. Can they feed the dog? Sort and fold laundry? It doesn't matter if they don't do a good job, it just matters that they are doing it.

Invite them into your schedule, and your day-to-day tasks. It might be faster, and easier to make dinner, and clean the kitchen without trying to involve your kids, but how much fun is that? Can they cut something up? Stir something? Taste something? Put something away?

If they can't help you, at least let them be around you. Give them some kitchen toys when you're in the kitchen. Some cleaning toys when you're dusting and vacuuming the living room. Let them do their part, while you do yours.

1. **Get outside! Get outside! Get outside!**

Never let a day go by when you don't get outside with your kids. Not only do kids need fresh air and open spaces, they need to explore nature. Go for a walk, and talk about the birds, trees, leaves and grass. Collect flowers, and leaves. Talk about the weather, and the seasons. Find some puddles to play in.

Don't let bad weather stop you from enjoying the outdoors. You might have to limit your time outside if it's really cold, really hot, or heavy rain, but other than that these days can be super fun. Don't be afraid to get muddy and wet, or to get your hands cold playing in the snow. These are often the experiences your kids will remember most.

1. **Bring the outside, in, and the inside out.**

Who says you can't break the rules? Try bringing in some mud to play with, or setting up the kid-sized pool on the kitchen floor? Sound scary, and messy. Well, it probably will be. Will your kids love you for it? Yes.

Clear a space inside your house and let them play with their outside toys, like big cars, and bikes.

Bring the inside out too. Take a blanket, and some books and read under that big tree at the park, or your back yard.

Build your own jungle gym, inside the house. Find boxes, and stepladders, and soft cushions to jump into.

Let them play with snow, inside the house. You just fill the bathtub with snow, and let them play, with their gloves on or off.

Make a picnic, in the middle of the living room. Let your kids bring something to the picnic. Sing songs, and dance around, eat something messy.

Take naptime, story time, lunchtime – outside!

Set up a tent inside the house. Let them sleep in the tent if they want, eat a snack in the tent, and play with you in the tent. Camping indoors is great anytime of the year!

1. **Find an indoor gym, or somewhere where they can run around, be loud, and get their sillies out, anytime of year.**

A lot of daycares have great outdoor spaces because they know how important this play is, but did you know they also almost always have access to a big, indoor play space? If your kids aren't in daycare, you need to find a space like this. Ask other moms, find a local community centre, and find a big space your kids can run around in when the weather doesn't cooperate.

1. **Put on some loud music, and have a family dance party.**

You need to have fun with your kids. And, it's always a great idea to start your own traditions too. Put on some of your favorite music, and teach them how to line dance, or boogie. Get those sillies out! Sometimes they just need to get their energy out to be able to focus. Try this before family mealtime. Maybe they'll be more focused afterwards.

Conclusion: Final Thoughts

Thanks for reading this book. We hope you have learned a lot, and incorporated positive parenting into your lives. As our little ones keep growing, there are more and more milestones that we have to accomplish. Starting school, becoming more independent, making friends... the world is an exciting place for our little ones. What's next?

Learning is such an exciting adventure for our little ones. They are super-curious, and ready for anything. Use your preschoolers' curiosity and sense of adventure for good – give them plenty of opportunities to try new things, eat new foods, and get into safe and fun trouble.

Don't forget to enjoy these years with your preschooler. Life moves fast, and we are always rushing to the next thing. Talk to parents whose kids have grown up and they all say the same thing, "It goes so fast". Remember that these preschool years are times to relish and enjoy.

As your preschooler starts school there will be many more

CONCLUSION: FINAL THOUGHTS

exciting challenges ahead. What can you do to get your preschooler ready, and excited about starting school? The first thing you can do is to get yourself prepared. If you are excited about starting school, they will see that. Take the time to prepare your preschooler by using some of the fun techniques in this book. Remember to take time to have fun and play too. Playing is how our little ones explore and learn about the world around them, and is the most important part of their day.

Thank you for purchasing and reading this book. Enjoy and celebrate each new experience with your preschooler, now, and in the future. We hope you making every day with your preschooler a special one! Enjoy!